WRITINGS FROM THE SPIRIT

Written By

PETER BENJAMIN LEBUHN

Order this book online at www.trafford.com
or email orders@trafford.com

Most Trafford titles are also available at major online book retailers.

Printed in the United States of America.

ISBN: 978-1-4269-5066-7 (sc)
ISBN: 978-1-4269-5067-4 (e)

Trafford rev. 01/17/2011

 www.trafford.com

North America & international
toll-free: 1 888 232 4444 (USA & Canada)
phone: 250 383 6864 ♦ fax: 812 355 4082

THE JOURNEY

Beleaguered and Beaten
Burned to a crisp
My faith I have lost
What is to become of this?
The Fire burns brightly...The ashes spread widely.
All I feel is death
Lord how do I get out of this?
The light flickers only dim
But flicker it does
For The answer now is known
I have lost everything only to regain it
Trials and toils
They do boil in the deep of my soul
My burning and yearning to do right
With all thy might
I humble thyself in thy sight
The journey has been long...now I am strong

Peter LeBuhn

PETER LEBUHN:A BIOGRAPHY

Peter LeBuhn: A Biography
Some say He is A simple man
Some Say Complex
Some say Full of Passion
Some Say Spirit Filled

A Gift Has Been Given
For Thee to Share with the
World
My Life
My Love
My Heart

Peter LeBuhn is all of these
His words speak volumes
Touch hearts
As he cares for others humbly
His Life is Not His Own
For He Is A Gift To The World
He only aims to please one Master
Jesus Christ

Peter LeBuhn
2002

A SECOND CHANCE

A Second Chance
To Dance
To Live...To Sing...To be thankful
And Give
I set apart this opulent opportunity
Not for myself
For I am put on the shelf
A second chance to serve
with a narrow faith
Ne'er to swerve
Once Fallen
Broken Wings
Now I understand to serve my King
All of My Heart
All of My Mind
All of My Soul
...A Second Chance
...A Second Chance

Peter LeBuhn
2006,2010

ALL THAT WAS HIDDEN...
ALL TO BE SHOWN

I come before thee
Naked
Bearing myself to you
with all of my soul to see
All that was hidden
All to be shown
It seems such a crime
Not to let it be known

Appearing before your glory
Blinded by your presence
and mastery

I come humbled before you
Lifted up on wings of eagles
You raise me.
Your grace...Your mercy
saves me
All that was hidden..All to be shown

Peter B LeBuhn

ANGEL OF LIGHT

Thy vision of light awaits
Visions lead to a discovery of the fantastic
Elegant Visions lead me
…to a luxurious marble hallway
…occupied with priceless works of art on the walls.
An angel in a sparkling golden dress walks towards the large wooden
door.
The door has a handle of rich silver
Surrounded by beams of moonlight, guiding to riches on the other side.
Watching without breath, the angel reaches for the silver.
suddenly a brilliant light flooded the hallway as the door began to open.
as if in harmony, a light of equal brilliance and intensity shone from a
silver pendant worn close to the woman's heart. This vision was so vivid
and real that it startled me from sleep… I knew that I had discovered
something of value.
The riches that lie behind the door are limitless
What treasures and delights does this incredible door hold for you,
Will it be a vault full of diamonds, rubies, and pearls? Will it be that
dream that has always eluded you? The riches, the prestige can all be
yours before you know it!

Mystical Power from the Ancients channel pulsating energy
In healing bringing forth what is desired
The power surge created by interlocking pyramids
Adorned in crystal and silver it shines
Now striding through that wooden door, head held high
With God's blessing

Peter LeBuhn 2010

BE ENCOURAGED

Be encouraged
Consider everything in every nature
A gift
Humble thyself
Not Displacing importance of your ownself
Exalting others before you
In Death There is Life
Ne'er an end in sight
Though on earth beaten and ravaged
He shines as the stars
Living in One Nations Hearts
In The End
Every knee bows
Every tongue confesses
You are the One True God
And Jesus Christ
Lord and Savior
Amen

Peter LeBuhn

Copyright 2010

BEACON OF LIGHT

You are my beacon of light
Your illumination lights my path
The trail I walk
The course I take
Unknown
My heart IS
Filled with Your Love
And Treasure for Creation
Your teachings are my Nation
Your ways Incarnation

My Beacon of Light
I have no Fright
You have made the darkness
Bright

One Scripture...One Christ
One Word...One God
ONE GLORY
The Five Solas
Forever Ring True

Peter LeBuhn

BEACON OF LIGHT (Spanish)

You are my Beacon of Light
(Usted es mi faro de la luz)
Your illumination lights my path
(Su iluminación enciende mi trayectoria)
The trial I walk
(El rastro camino)
The course I take
(El curso que tomo)
Unknown
(Desconocido)
My heart IS
Filled with Your Love
(Mi corazón se llena de su amor)
And Treasure for Creation
Your teachings are my Nation
Your ways Incarnation
(Y el tesoro para la creación sus enseñanzas es mi nación su encarnación de las maneras)
My Beacon of Light
I have no Fright
(Mi faro de la luz no tengo ningún fright)
You have made the darkness
Bright
(Usted ha hecho la oscuridad brillante)
One Scripture...One Christ
One Word...One God
ONE GLORY
The Five Solas
Forever Ring True
(Un Scripture... Una Palabra De Cristo Uno... Una GLORIA Del Dios UNO Los Cinco Solas Suena Por siempre Verdad)

Peter LeBuhn

BROUGHT ALIVE

Brought Alive by your beauty
To love you...My Duty
It is Just You and I
Your love you Supply

The walk down Chestnut Street
Makes me Feel Complete
Through the Campus our walk
As it goes from block to block

Hand in hand
Arm in Arm
In the Moment With You
You with me

These are the things memories are made of
These are the things memories are made of

Peter LeBuhn
Copyright ©2006 Peter B. Lebuhn

BUTTERFLY

Like a Butterfly
You rest on the evening star
...Where you are resting afar
This song which holds our spirits kindrid
Live From Day to Night

Many Struggles...
...Tears
...Embraces
The joy of something grand
A cultivated harmonious friendship
...With No Limits
...You A friend without blemish
...You stole my heart
Now I must make my stand
...These dreams
...These thoughts of you
Unexplainable
...What say you of me?
My precious butterfly
...Don't fly far
...Don't fly far

Peter LeBuhn

Peter LeBuhn

AN ANNIVERSARY SONG
(court of love)

An Anniversary Song
Answers In A Game Of Questions
After The Sensations
The Midnight Hour
Increases Thy Power
...Thy Love Heightened from above
Coming before thee
In your Court of Love
...Found Guilty
You sentence thee
To a lifetime of passion

By The River
...We Go
A care ne'er to take
Our love we partake
An Anniversary Song
Forever to be sung

Peter LeBuhn

Copyright ©2006 Peter LeBuhn

DREAMS, WHAT GREATNESS IS MADE OF!

A thought
A dream
A glimmer of light that takes Flight
In the middle of the Night
These are the things of Greatness
For time is of the essence
There can be no lateness
To reach the pinnacle
The time for action
is now
Do Not Bow
Take your dream into action
For it is with a thought
A Dream
that great things are built on! !
Freedom: Built on A Dream
We have America
Electricity: Built on A Dream
We have Heat
Dreams What Greatness is made of
Thoughts into action what Greatness is made of!

Peter LeBuhn
Copyright 2004

DEUCE GAME

For candy drue my lifelong friend

Is it Advantage In?
Is it Advantage Out?
Or Deuce?
Many Questions surround my heart
Unsure of what has been entered into
I know what I see
It is good and blessed
The direction yet to be seen
Many Questions
remain not asked
dancing delicately
in and around conversations
In time you will know
So we will go
and grow
My heart that is softening
No more questions will it surround
The questions that need to be asked
Soon will no longer remain.
It will be a deuce game equal partnership

Peter B LeBuhn
Copyright October 22, 2002

THE VOICE ON THE RADIO

For cyndy drue my favorite radio d.j.

Your voice on the Radio
Touches my heart so
Your voice from afar
speaks to me so near

I smile as I listen
As I nervously glisten

My Name for all the world to hear
Is this the beginning
Of something dear

Peter B LeBuhn
Copyright 2005

EN PARIS CES'T MA MAISON

En Paris Ces't Ma Maison
The Paris Skylight
Shines upon your rose room in the early morning.
Portraits of the sea
portraits of Monet and Renoir...serene
boating scenes

You saunter to your full-length mirror
you comb your soft silky hair.
Joy is in your heart...You have found
Paradise.

Your morning walk begins
You pass the Luxembourg Gardens
Le Belle fleur de jar din
A smile glistens off your face
The Arc De Trimphe...The symbol of Liberties de France

The beauty continues
with the Champs Elysees
and the Concorde

In Paris you have found your heart
your love
your home

Peter LeBuhn

EXPLORING A MYSTERY

Your smile
Brings the warmth of the sun to my heart
When we are apart
It is you I think of in blissful memory
for the rest of my days.

Your hair unfurled
In golden locks of glorious disarray
As the sun shines upon you.

Your eyes inviting
As we frolic near the water stream
Nearer you come to me
Beaming
Shining
Your beauty Blinding
Blinding you may be I cannot help but be
Hypnotized by your captivating beauty
I must have you...My heart pounds like a
drum. Happiness has entered my life.

Peter LeBuhn
Copyright 2002

FRUITS, FLOWERS, SATIN SHEETS

Fruits, Flowers,
Satin sheets
Branches of my heart
Beat for only One.
There is fear
Do not tear it with your hands,
Your beautiful eyes as they hypnotize
Your presence is soft.
It is not oft to meet such a prize.
Arriving morning dew
The wind comes to freeze thy face.
No matter... You are here with thee in this place.
Rest your silky feet..., Revel in these of moments dear
Your young centre let roll my sound
Toute head encor of your last kisses;
Let it calm down good storm,
And which I keep watch as you sleep and rest.

2006 Peter B. Lebuhn

GRACE AND HONOR

To You I give Grace
To You I give Honor
For you are the one
...That has allowed me to save face

In trials and turmoil's
Troubles and Boils
You are there
In all of this universe
There is no compare

The One True
You make my soul Anew

To you True
Obedience is mine
I am yours
Your ways I will climb

Peter LeBuhn

Copyright ©2006 Peter LeBuhn

Homage (A 911 Poem)

Terror in the eyes and ears of our country
A monument of 3,000 lives GONE
In a moment
Our lives stopped
In a moment
We could not reach the ones we loved
Tears run down my face
as the names are mentioned
From boyhood, a good friend
went to be with out Father in Heaven
He was 33
Phone Lines Down
My heart frowns
As I watch the planes dive into the
towers I cry more and more
Freedom it is worth fighting FOR

Peter LeBuhn

GREATNESS

Greatness falls upon thee
as the rain showers to a stormy day.
Many storms...weathered
Many trials...sustained
Lives touched
My spirit becomes stronger
My testimony reaches further
with each individual
This Greatness is a gift
From the Father
He gave me talents
and told me to water and nurture them
The seeds have grown
To many in His name.
Thank you Father
for this Humble Greatness
Thank You.

Peter B LeBuhn
Copyright 2005

HAPPENSTANCE

Meeting by Happenstance
Our eyes
pulled together
It is as if we know each other
Drawing near to a kiss
Entering a world of never ending
BLISS
The Fantasy Has begun
Our songs of passion will be
SUNG
We are writing our own story into
HISTORY
Each moment...each second
It is precious
Our Hearts warm as the Sun
Cool as the Waters
What has Begun
Never to End! ! !
Never to End! ! !

Peter B LeBuhn

HAPPY BIRTHDAY

Happy Birthday to You
Happy Birthday to You
Happy Birthday to Sweet and
Faithful You
Happy Birthday to You

Hi Julia,
Sweet Julia
My Sister in God
I bless the day he made you
May you have a peaceful happy and joyful anniversary of
your birth

In God we Trust

Peter LeBuhn

HARVEST FANTASY (VIZIONS)

The Day is dark
Rainy...and all so whet!
But with her
Life is illuminating
And warm

As we frolic in the rain
With all the passion and vigor
That our hearts can generate
Our arms wrapped around each other
With a tender embrace

The rain has ceased
The sun has risen
All the colors of the rainbow
Are upon us
As we lay in a mountain
Of colorful fall leaves

I look at her I know she is joyful
Because of the smile in her eyes
And the glow upon her face

Peter LeBuhn
Copyright 1998, 2010

HOLD ON

The moon shines bright
The stars overlooking above
On a clear night
We are separated afar

Do you think of me
Does your heart beat for thee
Hold On...Hold on Tight
To the One you Love.

Times of trial abound us
Temptations around
Hold On
Hold on Tight
You must believe what you have is true
Let's keep it simple
What we have will grow day by day
Week by Week Month by Month Year by Year
Hold On!
Hold On!

Peter LeBuhn
Copyright 1996,2010

I KNEW IT WHEN I SAW YOUR FACE

I knew it when I saw your face
I don't know your name
It makes no difference just the same

Do you believe in Love at First Sight?
I hope and pray
You Will Say
'I just might'
Do you believe then...
...In taking off into flight
I hope and pray you will say
'Outta Sight'

I knew it when I saw your face
I don't know your name
It makes no difference just the same

Not a word ever spoken
There is no need
Words our spoken in silence with our eyes
...With our minds
You and I...A breed of a special kind

Oh, how I long to make you mine
With you my rainy days shine
You make them feel oh, so fine
Oh, How I love to cuddle beside you by firelight

I knew it when I saw your face
Now that I know your name
It makes a difference just the same

Copyright ©2005 Peter B. Lebuhn

IN THE GROOVE OF THE NIGHT

In the Groove of the Night
Free of Fright
The Moon Shines Bright
Like a Spy

The tide Roars In
The exploration about to begin
I watch as this is Happenin'

In the Groove of the Night
The Portal of Passion found
Not Paying Attention to a sound

You Lost in Me
I in You

In The Groove of The Night
Our Passion Has Taken Flight

Peter LeBuhn

Copyright ©2005 Peter B. Lebuhn

IN YOUR EYES

In Your Eyes
The Future Is Seen
In Your Eyes
The road is clear and clean
In Your Eyes
There is Happiness and Joy
In Your Heart
Much Love to Give
Ne'er to Depart
In Your Heart
The More You Give
The Greater Reward
In Your Hands
You take Mine
In Your Hands
You Take Mine

Peter LeBuhn
Copyright 2006

JUNGLE LOVE

The time of year when Jasmine bloom,
most sweetly in the summer weather,
Helpless in the fragrant Jungle gloom,
On sultry night we spent together,
We, Love and Night, together blend,
A Trinity of tranced content.

Your lips belong to me, wholly mine.
To kiss...To Drink....To Caress
Hearing from afar in faint distress
Sweet Wine One of Great Love Potions
To Set In Motion
The Fullness of Your Delight
With Our Passion
There Is No Fright
Taken In Abandon
Quivering note of Human Tremor
To rise and fall again,
In Shouts of ecstasy throughout the night,

Tasting the perfumed flower
In the moonlit hours
Tasting of the Jasmine flowers.

Peter LeBuhn

KISS OF A LOVER

To be kissed by my lovers mouth
Her Kiss is sweeter than wine.
To savor the ointments poured fourth in love.
Thy Name is as ointment poured forth,
An ointment to the heart.
How much I love thee.
Draw me Nearer
To will I follow
Your Chambers I rejoice in gladness
Fruitful are our vines
Remember we will Days Gone By
Days To Come
The keeper of my vineyards
Come drink with me,
Thy cheeks are rows of jewels,
Thy neck shines like gold.
Keep my vineyards with me
Behold, thou art fair
My love
A vision to behold,
With doves eyes
They do hypnotize.
This love Is One Love
To Be Lived in Much Love

LA BELLE DE LE TERRE

La Belle De Le Terre
Ma, Etre en amour
Ce'st un joile a la terrase
d'un cafe de amour

Je Parlez avec vous
Amour en mon couer
Venez Ici! ! !
Je Vous Appeler
Vous Regarder moi facon

Je fuir a elle
Tremper ma avec grande baisers
Peter LeBuhn

Copyright ©2000 Peter B. Lebuhn
Peter LeBuhn

Copyright ©2005 Peter B. Lebuhn

LAST OF THE GOLDEN BOYZ

My hey day
Time to make my noise

When you embark
Make your mark
...Shine...Shine
Show your spark

Let the World know
You are always going to
Hit a New Plateau

To have a flair
...To care
A clinician
With a mission

Last of the Golden Boyz
Shine...Shine You will receive your shrine

Copyright ©2000 Peter B. Lebuhn

LIVE WIRE

Things going on Here and There
Things going on everywhere
Living in a world of craziness
Seems like life is a scare
Living on a Live wire
Never sure when it is going to overload

Can't let it break me
Can't let is shake me
Got-ta beat the world at its' own game

Seems it's always been the same
Life is a crazy mixed up game
You have got to know who to listen to
You have got to play carefully
...Or you may end up
...Living on a Live Wire

Can't let it break me
Can't let is shake me
Got-ta take on the world
Got-ta beat the world at its' own game

Peter LeBuhn
Copyright ©2000 Peter B. Lebuhn

LOVE

I just want to look into your eyes.
I want to feel your warm breath.
I want to see your smile and know that this smile is for me.
I want to be waken up by you rather than some kind of alarm clock.
I want to be your sunshine.
I want you to warm your hands up in the back pockets of my jeans.
I want you to pay me with your kisses for the rental of my jeans pockets.
I want to belong to you and. I am yours and you're mine.
I want to believe you and never question anything you say.
I want to hear your voice. I want to get to your inner thoughts.
I want to be everything you need. I want you to know all these things.
I want you to love me.
Can't wait for the moment I board the plane and start my final journey to you.

Peter LeBuhn

LOVE AT FIRST SIGHT

Feelings That I have No Control, No Power
As I stand before Thee In the Wild Flower.
Thy will is strong but overruled by Love and
Joyous Spirit.
Thy Emotions
Taken by Your Sweet Potion.
We are stripped, unclothed
Let the course of Love begin.
The Exploration...Impending
Where to start...Where to End
Two Flowers Budding
...Growing Together
The reason for this affaire
This ceremonial occasion
No man could Dare know
Behold Thee in Mine censured eyes
You My Love...To my surprise
Deliberate the love we make...and take
Who ever loved
There is love at first sight

Peter LeBuhn

LOVE IN MANY LANGUAGES

Hola
Bonjour
Ciao
Hallo
Las cosas del amor le traigo cosas del amor que le doy
Des choses de l'amour je vous apporte des choses de l'amour
que je vous donne
Cose di amore porto voi le cose di amore che dò voi
Sachen der Liebe hole ich Ihnen Sachen der Liebe, die ich
Ihnen gebe
Love in many languages
Love in many languages
The one language we all understand is love

Peter LeBuhn

LYRIC OF A LOVE SONG

The Lyric of a Love Song
Beats Softly on my heart
Unexpected Feelings
Could this be the healing

The hot sun beats down
Flowers all around
A connection...A friendship made
A year has passed since we saw
One another
Same time Next Year We say
Yet closer than ever
What we have will never sever

The way you look at me
As we sit and talk
in a Philadelphia Bar
Bruno's on Pine
This is an Amazing moment in time
Truly an Amazing moment in time

Peter LeBuhn

LYRICAL VERSES

Spilling lyrical verses
Keeping you warm
Your mind
Your thoughts
...Entranced
...At Every Glance
The lyrics I spill
bring thee closer
Feeling the warmth of your breast against mine
Whispering Secrets of Love in our ears
It appears
There is something here
You Lost in Me
I, You

They are the danger of Love
And the Pleasure of all things above

Peter LeBuhn

MIDNIGHT HOUR

The midnight hour
Thy moon high
Thy stars 'nigh
Willingly venturing into an unknown

Lights adorn the cobblestone streets
A little, little boy, plays feutball in yon churchyard past,

On all around their beauteous radiance cast,
This midnight hour.
All is quiet
Yet their is a riot
One that cannot be heard
Not a Word

Journeying o'er the path of life,
Onward, forward we move
With stars and northern lights o'er head in strife,
Perfect Bliss
Is This
The stars are out
For me
This midnight hour.

Rising High Does the full moon
Saying Hello to the Night
All of her shine and luster

Bursting through the darkness wherein she was enshrined;
Arise, Arise
Willing, active, rapid thought
The past is the past as it intertwines the future
At midnight hour.

2006 Peter LeBuhn

MUSIC HALL FUNK

The moon has risen
Venturing down a dark back alley
The night is misty

In the far off distance
Hearing music
....people playing
....people singing
....people dancing

It is a music hall
down a cobblestone street
Slipping in the side door
The music overtakes me
....into a fierce dancing beat

Noticing two ladies by the bar
checking me
Playing to them and dance increasingly seductively

They are coming upon me
The dream has begun
The fantasy...Set in Place
....The dance we will make
....The future is ours is to see
....The future is ours to take

Peter LeBuhn

MY ANGEL

Coming into my life
On a breeze
One cool September eve
You found the door of my heart
and began to play
Beautiful music...I heard
at the start
Lightly I could hear the pitter pat of the drums
as you would talk with me
Then as the conversation continues
In comes the string quartet
Beautiful Music
My Angel
Seeing you from across the room
For you now I swoon
I live for you
I love for you
You are my reason
You are my Angel

Peter LeBuhn Copyright 12/5/2006

MY CHINA ROSE

The cold wind blows
In the white of the snow
catching a glimpse of you
walking like a china rose

I testify
To the heights of the sky
You I cannot let fly by

This china rose
The way she looks at me
With a certain prose
My heart glows

Her smile
Has made it all worthwhile
My China Rose

MY FIRST LOVE

I met you at Cafe de Margots
A beautiful sunny morning in Paris
Me...The American man in a foreign land
You...The belle of the land.
We talked and spoke of life and love
You took my hand and made your stand.
'Meet me at L'Hotel D'Paris' you said
Fearful I paused but my heart said yes.
I agree.
The hour approaches
I am wearing the colours of your country
Blue jacket, white pants, red striped shirt.
WOW! My heart beats as I see you
wearing your turquoise taffeta sundress.
We are to dine at L'Tour de Eiffel
I am living a dream
I offer to pay...She insists she must
for she asked me. We venture down the
streets of Paris We embrace in a waterfall.
You taught me the meaning of Love.
Walking Hand in Hand...Arm In Arm
Approaching The Hotel Of Paris
Dripping Whet
Ascending to the room
Undressing and Drying each other off passionately...
simultaneously

You wear my white cotton dress shirt and a beautiful pink
thong
Putting the Beautiful French Music On.
Sabrina...You Dance Around Me
Take Me in Your Arms
This Man in a Foreign Land...Fallen Prey to your charms.
We Make Love all night inside each others silken bodies.
The morning comes early
Things to do...Studies ahead
Understanding that this may come to an end
'Sabrina I understand if you are not here when I return'
Responding quickly 'No, No I will be here I want to be with
you'
Sabrina, Thank you
For You Have taught me what Love Is
You Have Taught Me What Love Is.

Peter B LeBuhn
Copyright 1983, 2010

MY POTION

The sun radiates her beams upon the sand
This world, truly grand
The quietness of the ocean
The tide in forward motion
It is my potion.

Vizions of Dolphin
Swimming 'fore me
Nothing compares
To this feeling from within.

Alone in the vast creation
As life was meant to be
This spiritual sensation
The sights, smells and sounds

By the hands of what stylist could have painted this picture?
What Genius?
What Virtuoso?

Giving Thanks for this creation
with feeling of elation.

Humbled, feeling modest
In a world so large and powerful.
Grateful for this Gift To enjoy.

Peter LeBuhn

NATURE IN ALL HER FLAVOUR

This song was written on the shores of corolla light ,north Carolina, thanksgiving 2005

Nature
(In all her flavor)
Silently speaks
through her radiant beauty

She greets each day with a sense of duty
Rising over the horizon
The sun slowly awakes
O'er the unfettered waters
Singing in Each day with new Psalters.

Nature
(In all her flavor)
Silently speaks
through her radiant beauty

The Landscape Framed by
Green Pine and Fur Trees
Sights and Sounds of the seagulls
In their home.
The banging of the water on the shores
Sights of the sea white water
as it fiercely rolls in.

Nature
(In all her flavor)
Silently speaks
through her radiant beauty

The white sands
through my toes
The wind in my hair
The fresh sea air

Nature
(In all her flavor)
Silently speaks
through her radiant beauty

Peter LeBuhn

Copyright ©2005 Peter B. Lebuhn

PEACE

_**This song was written in 75 minutes on a trip to
Baltimore, MD.**_

Speak to me of serenity, of treasures yet to be found, of peace
that flows
like a river. Tell me of tranquil places that no hand has
marred, no storm
has scarred. Give me visions of standing in sunlight or the
feeling of
spring mist against my cheek as I live and move and breathe.
Show me paths
that wind through the wild lilies and beds of buttercups. Sing
me songs like
the mingled voices of wrens and meadowlarks, the lowing of
gentle cows, the
soft mother-call of a mare to her colt. Lead me past a glass-
smooth pond
where frogs croak of coming-out parties, their graduation
from frisky
tadpoles to squat green frogs. Find me a place in the sunlight
to sit and
think and listen to the sweet inner voice that says so quietly,
'Peace, be
still.'

Peter LeBuhn 2008

OH WHAT A WORLD

Oh What A World
She takes me for a twirl
Accidental encounters
Crystal counters
Oh What A World
Every significant moment
Vital...In the blink of an eye
Life Changing...With Nature's Wind
Every Decision made.
Oh What A World
Life takes us for a twirl
Life-Saving, Life -Altering
Appreciation for what is given.
Bestowed upon thy world my love.
It is A gift from above
Oh What A World
Continents collide
So Far in Destination
Yet so close in ideology
So Close Yet So Far
So Far Yet So Close

Copyright ©2005 Peter LeBuhn

OUR HEARTS UNCHARTED

You smile to Me From afar
Your name It is unknown
My heart warms to roaring flame.
The drum beats become louder by the
Second.

Still, you do not speak
Yet you are inviting me into
your world.
A WORLD of the Unknown
Many Pages will be written
On blank sheets from our hearts.

The course of this story is
uncharted. No one else has
read our book. Not even us.
I will find out who you are
and as for the pages. The first
Entry will be You.

Copyright ©2005 Peter B. Lebuhn

Paris I adorent

France, her mystery
Her history
Around each corner
A story unfolds

The quietness of La Seine
The elaborateness of Le Tour Eiffel
Paris I ado rent
As it is you I explore
We have developed rapport

En Paris ces't ma couer
En Paris ces't ma maison

One day we will meet again
One day we will meet again

Peter LeBuhn
Copyright 1996, 2010

PEACE IN A HECTIC WORLD

The Cold Wind Blows
It speaks loudly as I venture along.
The autumn leaves are falling.
A reminder that Winter
Soon will be here
I try to keep my heart warm
though reminders of death
all around me
The leaves have fallen
The cold has set in.
But Wait! ! !
There is beauty all around me
All of creation
a gift from thee
The deer and the animals they run about.
The streams and the rivers running.
Almost speaking silently...peacefully
Truly in this hectic world
There is peace
There is peace

PLEASURES OF THY HEART

My Love Come to be with thee
The pleasures of our hearts will prove
Valleys Green
Rolling in the Groves and Fields

By Shallow Waterfalls
I sing to thee my Songs
Doves circle above in approval
As your golden locks unfurl
In the rose petals 'neath us

Your eyes pull thine closer
Closer to you...Not a word
Yet you speak loudly with your heart

These pleasures of our hearts
Ne'er to part
These pleasures of our hearts
Struck by the Loving Dart.

Copyright ©2005 Peter B. Lebuhn

PUERTO RICO

You are in my stocking hung with care
Sights of Puerto Rico... Outside are there
Whoooooooooooosing Waves
The sea breeze
Just you and me
All that matters... you and me
Diamonds in your eyes
I have made you mine
Traveling through the ruins of the city
The churches... the castles
The Museums... Paintings of El Greco Adorn
Living a dream
near an island stream
Hypnotized by your eyes
Your touch
Your love
Your tenderness

Copyright ©2005 Peter B. Lebuhn

RHYTHMS OF THE NIGHT

Seduced by the rhythms of the night
Sounds of People Laughing
People Singing
People Dancing
Entices me nearer to the source
The night streets covered in fog
I venture down the cobblestone streets
to find the source
The sounds of the street beat
that move my feet
The music emanates from a dark alley
through a side door.
The music Pumping...Thumping
set afire by the music
The music and my soul become one
My feet dance aflutter
Shutter I think to what the future holds
As you and I embrace into one body
Engulfed into One
Nothing around us matters
Just You and I

Copyright ©2005 Peter B. Lebuhn

SILENCE

Silence Golden
In this moment
Though the silence

Many thoughts are spoken
Something happening
A strange occurrence
that cannot be unbroken

Your smile stretches a mile
Bright as the sun
Blinding...Yet I go nearer
Thy heart becomes undone
It becomes clearer

You are the One
You are the One

SING A NEW SONG!!!

Singing to each new day a new song
Sing out Strong
Thy Life, it is thy song
Thy song is thy gift

The gift to be given to everyone
All across the earth
A song for all nations
Tribes, tongues

Songs of honour and majesty
will be sung
Joyous sounds from many lungs
Man, Woman, Child

Rejoice, Again Rejoice
'Let the Heavens be glad and the earth rejoice;
Let the sea roar, and all that fills it' (Psalm 96: 11)

The skies will open up
The brightness will blind us
This is the day we meet our Lord
Our Creator
Our Savior

Copyright ©2005 Peter B. Lebuhn

SLICE OF TIME

Sailing Through Life
On A Breeze
Entering in
A Beautiful woman
Stealing part of my life
Taking this slice
Making it hers
With her pirate smile

heart being stolen
thoughts on the girl
Unsure what will unfurl
That Slice of time
You own from me

Slice of time
Precious
In the right place at the right time
The right woman
The right man....

On A Breeze
On A Slice
A single second
Changes our whole life

Peter LeBuhn

SPANISH EYES

In your eyes
A pleasant surprise
You steal my heart
You I will not depart

My Systems Are Go
As we embark on our mission of love

In your arms
Warm and close
Your Heartbeat against mine
You are thine

In my mind
You are there
All the time

My life
My love
My loyalty
For you

Copyright ©2004 Peter B. Lebuhn

The Dance

In the hills of green
And the Sunshine's sheen
Like a panther...your beauty
and grace came about thee
without a warning...without a
trace.
Entranced by your charms
You are like royalty
Humble wearing your arms.
Words are not spoken
It is understood
The dance has begun
The future is love

Peter B LeBuhn
Copyright ©2004 Peter B. Lebuhn

THE DANCE ETERNAL

Marvelous and graceful
Plentiful breasts
Beautiful posterior
Shaved soft and silky
She is beautiful
Stargazing her belly dance
Sensuous movements of the hips
Watching her body
Maneuvering to the melody
Arching her back
Tossing her hair
She is dancing, prancing for me
Kissing me with her eyes
As I kiss her with mine
She is nearly through
Following her to the back
Waiting for her to follow
It does not take long
I grabbed a handful of her hair...with passion
Pulling her bosom to mine French kissing her
Soft and gentle at first
Then not so soft
Sliding my tongue down her body
Taking my time at her nipples
On her belly, on her clit
Plunging my tongue into her treasure

She tasted sweet and tart all at once
Sliding my fingers into her tight body
She tensed as I caressed her g-spot
Nursing on her clit
Feeling her body rock
Seeing her eyes roll in passion....in pleasure
Hearing her cries of X-T-C
Her body spasm
Silken ribbons of her nectar ran down my chin
Climbing her body kissing her deeply
Letting her taste herself on my tongue
She would dance for me again
The Dance Eternal

Peter LeBuhn

The Expressionless Page

The Expressionless Page
To an expressionless page
My pen takes action
The words of my heart flow
with passion.
A story is being written
A drama
A comedy
A tragedy (I hope not)
For in my heart
I know what is real
and true.
Every moment...Every second
The pen is making a new entry
The page now has meaning
and feeling
History is being made.
Where will my pen take me
The future will be seen.

THY FAITHFUL SERVANT

Thy Beloved
Invisible thy to you
You to I
Yet Bound by our Fathers love on High
All of these bodies.
Make Up …One Nation…Under God
There is no true life without the Father
The Son
The Holy Spirit
His Spicket
Drenches us in his Love
He Loves Every One
Why Then, Do You Search for answers?
The answer is clear
Christ is saying to you
I AM HERE! ! !
The quest within you
from whence born again
The transformation was to begin
Walking in Blind Faith
Though Seeing More Clearly
The Lord Is By Our Side
He is Our General
To Lead us in our battles
We strive for Perfection
Falling short of His Grace Each Time

Knowing We are Human Accepts Us Lovingly
He Stretches out his hands with the mighty key of Love
Faith Hope Love
The Greatest of these is Love He said
This is How my Father in Heaven Lived
So Shall I
By opening the door, you shall wake the Father.
Well Done Good and Faithful Servant! ! ! !
Well Done! ! !
Peter LeBuhn

THE FORBIDDEN KISS

The sweet aroma, fragrance of Thy indulgent fantasies
Your shadow, sexy silhouette approaches
...In the midnight hour
Frightened yet excited.... drawing closer
closer you take me into your body and soul
Longing for the kiss..
The forbidden Kiss
The forbidden fruit... that only your kiss does hold
Gazing at each others cherry lips with total astonishment
As if hypnotized...Drawing nearer...Closer
Longing for them to meet mine
Seeking to drink them in like a fine wine
This kiss...This Forbidden Kiss...So Sweet...Never Ending
Tasting the taste of raspberry wine
so splendid... on your lips
Interlocked in each others Arms...Legs
Forever Will This wonderful kiss
Be sought
Knowing, Hoping
Forever will be Forbidden

Copyright ©2005 Peter LeBuhn

THE GIFT OF LIFE

The Gift of Life
Ours to treasure
In all its splendor

The gift given from above
With Free Love
The Responsibility of the Gift Lay
With Us
To Confess
His Success
The Gift of Life
When I wake up
I taste of the Lords' Loving Cup
'This is the day the Lord Hath Made'
'Rejoice' 'Rejoice' and be Glad in it
For this life He has carefully knit
Everything that happens seems to fit
The Gift Of Life
I owe to My God...My Father
My Lord in Heaven

Peter LeBuhn

THE KEY TO YOUR HEART

Let me find the key to your heart so I can unlock your secret chambers of love when I do find that key, I will lock myself in your heart forever..

Peter LeBuhn

THE LIVING SONG

Sing a new song everyday
Live your song
For the song comes from deep within
You are the song
Sing it
Sing it
Loud like Thunder
The seas will part
The heavens will open
In pleasing
Sing a New song
Sing a New song

Peter LeBuhn

MAGIC OF LOVE
IN THE MOONLIGHT

Seeing you from a distance,
Dressed in cool white
The sweet curves of your body shine through
At long last our meeting
Our eyes
How they glisten
Outlined against the shimmering sands.
Getting closer to each other
The Stars how they shine into a myriad
of twinkling lights celebrating in harmony with joy as
they felt love wafting between us.

Very close to you
No room between us
Seeing a smile from those ruby lips, inviting a kiss.
Taking you in my arms and gaze deeply in your eyes.
The look of love, Desire
Wanting…Needing
The warmth of your body
Against the beat of thy heart.
Kissing gently at first,
Lips brushing each others.
A tap dance into passion
Knowing we cannot resist.
Your lips part

Our tongues dance together,
kissing deeper and with passion.
My heart bats faster.
Our senses command
Our bodies Demand
As we lie on the white sands,
the waves lapping at our feet, I ask, 'Shall we swim my
darling? 'Shall we swim in Love'

Copyright ©2006 Peter B. Lebuhn

The ones that got away!
The one that stayed

Lived a life of Lost Loves
Scars across my body
From each woman who has poisoned me
Still...My love for the fairer sex remains.

All of you got away
In Search of Love I say?
Wait a minute! ...Someone new?
Peering across a smoke filled room
The Glimpse of you in the alley

You stop...You look at me with your
Beautiful Brown Eyes
The message is clear
In your hesitation
You are the one that will stay

Peter LeBuhn

THE OPEN DOOR

The open door
Many times clouded by our
blind sight...We cannot see
This door never closes for it
is our way of future opportunity
The rain may fall
Our life may stall
The door is our vision to go on
Walk through the door
Questions will be answered
Your life will become clear
What is my purpose for being here?

Peter B LeBuhn

THE QUIETNESS OF MY HEART

I see you in the quietness of my heart
Your presence is felt with every beat
Your smile...Your radiance
shines from across the room blinding me
in a frenzy of warm happiness.
This day we are to spend together
In the midst of our hearts
Our minds...Our thoughts
In one accord.
Happiness has entered me at last
At last I am happy

Peter LeBuhn

THE SPIRIT WITHIN

The Spirit in me meets the same Spirit in you
saluting the divine in you
saluting the Light of God in you.
bringing together my body and soul,
focusing my divine potential,
bowing to the same potential within you.
bowing to the divine in you.
recognizing that within each of us is
a place where Divinity dwells,
when we are in that place, we are One.

Peter LeBuhn

THE TEACHER

Are you the Teacher?
...The question is asked
...Yes...Yes is the Response
A cold wind blows
A bus suddenly pulls forward
What is about to happen
...Life changing
Off the Bus
Approaches the Son
The Teacher, The Father Responds
Arms open wide
My son! My son!
You have come home
Where you belong
Next to the Fathers Side

Peter LeBuhn

THE TIGRESS
(LONELY IN THE NIGHT)

The Tigress
Lonely in the Night
Her Mate Away For a Journey
Longs for His Return
Dreaming
Thoughts of the touch
She loves so much
The smooth caress against her body
The 'Purring' against her neck
The passion and love
Between the two
Cannot be matched
No other above
The tiger will come home
From far off
Slowly approaching
...The Tigress
....Her head lifts...she knows his scent
They are together again at long last
At long last
There will be love
Once Again

Peter LeBuhn

THE VESSEL

Put on earth as a Vessel
To be used for His will
Every move that is made
will determine the future
How our time will be filled

The Word to be preached
In the way we live our lives
Our Talents we nurture
Help them to grow

Without the Utterance of your Name
People see you in your people
Through our works you will see our
Faith and Our Love For God Above
The talents we have our gifts from God
How we use them our gift to him

Peter B LeBuhn

Theatre of the Unknown

I saw you out of the corner
of my eye
gnashing your teeth
Looking almost half way shy
I know I saw you before
I can't place it where
Maybe in that bar
Or was it that night under the stars
Are you following me
Should I speak
You peer at me
You make not a peep
Only can I imagine your thoughts
when the smoke is cleared
You disappear
Once Again
This has been a
Theatre of the Unknown!!!

Peter B LeBuhn

THESE DREAMS

These dreams of these, So genuine, So true

You and I, delight, in a horse and carriage
ride on a winter day in the city, as we ride.
Along the boulevard, the wind is gusting
The trees, they are dancing in the wind

These dreams of these, So genuine, so true

Sauntering along the city sidewalks
We are talking, we are laughing
Sometimes just the gift, of each others presence
Just knowing that each other is there

These dreams of these, so genuine, so true

Candlelight dinners
Sitting close by fireside

These dreams of these
So genuine, so true

Peter B. LeBuhn

THOUGHTS OF YOU
WRAP AROUND MY SOUL

Thoughts of you wrap around my soul
With you on my mind
I lose control
Subdued by your passion
Conquered by your charms
Melting in your arms
...Thoughts of you wrap around my soul
This love has set off fire alarms
Wanting to hold back
But forth ventured
into the sexual unknown
This love we shall not postpone
Rushing in...like a tornado
A climatic zone
...Thoughts of you wrap around my soul
Wrapped around my soul
These thoughts will live
Forever

Peter LeBuhn

TIMELESS

The hour is timeless
Still
Caught in a moment
A fire has been lit to the wick
of our Passions.
Our hearts smoldering with each smile
Each glance
The heat...It does increase
Our hearts cannot part
The fire is ablaze.
Caught up now in each others arms
The world outside does not matter
Engulfed in Each others Passions
Drenched in Each others Love
A Timeless Treasure we are living
A gift of each other to each other

Peter B LeBuhn

TO SERVE

Not to swerve
To strive
For the Most High
Not to Yield
My faith...Is my shield
Your ways...My ways
For my Father
The Distance I will go
I will Follow
You are at my side when I feel
Hollow
To succeed is not of my doing
It is full faith in the Father
That Guides Me
Through My Life
Father you have released me from
My strife
You have released me from my strife

Peter LeBuhn

TO THE WHITE SEA

The journey is made
Being drawn nearer
Life choices become clearer

Feet sinking in the white sands
The moon and the stars
Looking down
Speaks volumes in the quietness of my heart
The roar of the tide
Opens up my mind

What Stylist? What Genius?
Painted a land such as this.
Alone in the eyes of my maker
Humbled
Feeling Small
In Awe
Of this great gift He has given me
Most of All

Peter LeBuhn

WAITING

Waiting
dressed as a lady in waiting
You come unto me
In the mist of the night
The river so bright
The moon shines above
smiling on the stars
The tide roars in
almost speaking in voice
On the sand
You approach
Through a cloud of fog
First your legs
Then your arms as they swing
Followed by your glorious body
with a mysterious smile
You come upon me not stopping
We are engulfed
The TWO...ONE
Waiting No more

Peter LeBuhn

Copyright ©2005 Peter B. LeBuhn

WHEN NIGHT BECOMES DAY

When Night Becomes Day
When Darkness Turns to Light
The Cold Wind concedes to the Warmth
The Passion...The Heat...The Affection
...Rises
...When Night Becomes Day
Two worlds collide
A soiree of emotion
Pours into a bottomless Love potion
...When Night Becomes Day
The coolness of the Night
Cool breeze against our Naked Hide.
Embraced under a moonlit Night
Everything to Confide
Deep Inside We know there will be no Divide.
It is now Day... The warmth of the Sun
Beams our Hide...We Smile at each other
No one shall come asunder
When two worlds collide
When Night Becomes Day

Peter LeBuhn

WITHOUT WORD

Dedicated to the woman who has inspired me, she knows who she is.

Without word you left for a far off land
... Without a plan...You Left... I waited and cried for you
What were you going to do?

When the news hit the front page.
... My heart shipwrecked... to the bottom of the sea

Without word
You left for a far off land
... Without a plan
I worried and cried for you
What were you going to do?

I searched the world over
But I found no trace
... Honey where are you hiding your beautiful face
I will be there to ease your pain
I will make you the center of my world
... And maybe make you happy awhile.

Wherever you are in that far off land
... I am with you
... I am with you
We will meet again-I know we will meet again

Peter B. Lebuhn

WONDROUS LIFE

What a wondrous life is this I lead
From my heart love does bleed
...My life I live for thee
...My love I give to thee

My Garden of fruitful mystery
and splendor
You will enter

You take me by the hand
Around each corner
....A new surprise
....To Find

What a wondrous life is this I lead
From my heart love does bleed
Peter LeBuhn

Copyright ©1999,2010 Peter B. Lebuhn

YOUR TOUCH MEANS SO MUCH

Looking into Your Eyes
Feeling Love gushing throughout my heart
At first glance
I know you are the one.
In my heart, Is this intense passion or emotion?
Now Knowing this love is genuine

Your touch means so much
Won't you come hug me
Won't you come love me

Come along with me
We will run hand in hand In fields so green.
We share precious moments together
We lay by the fire in the winter
We hold each close

Your touch means so much
Won't you come hug me
Won't you come love me

Your sensitivity fills me with joy when I am down
You are like a princess who wears a crown
Life is so much more wonderful while you are in my world
From all this you must be able to tell
I love you

Your touch means so much
Won't you come hug me
Won't you come love me

Peter LeBuhn

Copyright ©2005 Peter B. Lebuhn